YEAH, NO

12·20·23

Yeah, No

*For Sam,
with gratitude.*

Jordan Davis

Jordan

MadHat Press
Cheshire, Massachusetts

MadHat Press
MadHat Incorporated
PO Box 422, Cheshire, MA 01225

The Library of Congress has assigned
this edition a Control Number of
2023937819

ISBN 978-1-952335-61-7 (paperback)

Words by Jordan Davis
Cover photo: *Corn Truck Kingston Direct* © 2023 Tim Davis
Cover design by Marc Vincenz

www.MadHat-Press.com

First Printing
Printed in the United States of America

for New York

its indifference
and its change

Table of Contents

A Playground in Belize

Independence is for
the anonymous

Cops rolling backwards
on the shoulder
to the aid
of some troubled surfers

Waving my hoe
at the passing
red-wings?

Cat comes shaking
its head for
meatloaf

I feel so
unaware of the
telephone
I'm dialing
it's the wrong
time-of-day
to call
out in my sleep

Have nothing to say
is nothing to do

Every put-away thing
stays so criss-crossed

Red bird goes by
a narrow window
This bright clear red
goes into my body

It's like time stole your watch

Mockingbirds are
gray and white with
no mockings

And all the books say
Delay delay delay

Bad Poem

Put that rock down

In the Monkey

Hundred pounds of lead in the knapsack of your lust.
Dream every night of a girl in the park
eating her lunch, trying to gain weight, you love her,
she's thrilling! She looks straight ahead.

Corn Cakes

Corn cakes,
why do you make me sad?

A Little Poem

What energy took over our house
that we cleaned it all night
after such a pleasant dinner?

Heart

My heart wants
to ride a boat
It wants other things too
but to be on a boat under a bridge
with grasses barely breathing

Cotton of time darling corkscrew

In velvet settle all steam yawning

I love you and your latin midterm

Brown Paper

Lirica del Novecento.

Phone Call for Jones Very

Try being chosen, or not, sometime;
it entitles you to how your mother
held you, sang, etc. The church of
who you fall in love with in a clearing
smells of roses, lilacs, something sour,
a fugue meshes with the chemical
confusing you to murmur. All
the ether feels the pulse that carries you,
cornered by nightbirds, strong stranger.

Loud Singing

Believing me, believe me, be believing me.
I found the envelope empty.
I did not know I was not supposed to open the envelope.
He follows her up the stairs, she has white blonde hair.
What was going on inside the envelope?
A burst at the edge. Of light, the page.

You still

know what distance
to keep from the great
mistakes of our time

The Apricot

The red and white folded with gray
shadows of the American flag
reflected and beating in the concavity
of the silver orange bowl three seeds
ridged with spikes of here red here
orange dried fruit the spikes like
the edge the edge like the shell
of a crab the damp gray day
left at the isthmus the apricot

Up to Ten

Picked up and dropped
In rocks
     gold-fingered
     she stops
    A pyramid pushed,
    looking up
      brick
        nothing

Happy Baby

In the park in a carriage
dressed like (a little) your mother
the sun speaks to you
and you talk back
so fast the sun says
"I'm sorry?"

The Lost Poem

What cash
　　do you eager
　　　　to smile
　　the moves.

The cat
to words
　　　as bottle
　　of soda
is beaming
　　its pure mud—

"Sure, sky."

Anguish

A window shakes like a glasses
    blue and cloudy
The sun comes on
Bright   the clock tower
And the apartments
    the ventilator
The clocktower is gray again
The ventilator   white triangle
Birds walk lifting their wings
      down. The line
And the window, the threads
Blue. A swift

To a Sour Ball

The wired girl
with knapsack
strapped to the
middle of her
back, leaning
forward at
the light like
a jurist, hurries

A Bee

Blackcurrant juice is. Left
east and remote, silver
floating on a window a million.
inches over the hill.
Call, call,
a tarpaulin pillow. The win.
Relax under that
of it plays the laundry.
The sweep.

Hidden Poem

In the window in the shade of a blinder on a horse of porcelain
sewn into a shirt with stripes among miners in the outback
under the sofa behind pillows under blankets in a clear box
across your chest in the psalter on a branch in a wig at church
in the basement among wood
with the clouds on cold people at the farm in a bread bag
in a pile in the middle of the room in plain sight
below a flat roof with a gutter in a snowed-under car in a shoe
in an egg
down the left column on a prison calendar in love
by the ruins in the budget
in rhyme indoors by the hawk nests
underneath the tea service in poison ivy with an accent
along the guard rail in a filling elsewhere in your ear

The Very Plain Question

The working title of the face.

A Boat

I'm rowing you across a river in Banff, and when I
take you in a car to your mother's house, the Bay of Fundy.
At work the coast guard, walking there the merchant
marine, me in my pea coat.

You

Yawn ink store four
o'clock
they say trick the sun
dogs
biting under the
picnic tables
one brown one white
and brown these
trash can lids you
see them on the needles
of gauges

Always-Already

Ears as the train comes out
of the tunnel. The one One rings
a little hunting tune.
"What we call 'subject'
"Is not the unfathomable X,
"The ultimate reference point."

Complete thought arches
over the map like a diamond—
forehead against the window
in the harbor of the sky.

Saber-Toothed

The Ovids of rent star drawing
on cigarette ink design a reggae car
ruffles going. Past.

Is that filing cabinet a grand
mother a lantern in deep water post
mark and penny dining
room table money. The cape dimes of hot elastic
running saxophone freak

the passport in the flowers, oh
there was ballet and white
on the doors we like you.

Autumn like pure oxygen
on its starting line dream of the tone
in the county where she learned how to read.

Market Day At The Old House

Printing press in the clock,
and half-mast civilians come running
lipsticked.
Lost like a singer I stood
in a horse car,
the clarinet is who you are.

The hanging flowers reflect on you
and the canoe you print, $1.25
takes your uno to the sloppy model shop
when a leg's kicked up
like the bottom in jeans
its transcendental mezzanine
the lightship forgot,
lunchboxes rising
past kelp odoramas and bigots of sleep—
the video seagulls hollering closer—
May on the piers.

Cassiopeia

So far
they haven't moved,
the wall,
the boys
down the hill,
green shade
of the curtains
on the lady
crying in bed
with a fever,
so far
the five stars
haven't left
their omega,
Anna,
in bed
with a flower,
a pink
zinnia.

A Symposium

When I think
of Aristophanes
walking through
the woods
of northern
ancient times
coming across
two twined lovers
and tapping them
with a finger—

Kisses on Your Breast

Kisses on your breast like moths on a window
Kisses on your breast like a strawberry in the grass
Kisses on your breast like jackets on a chair
Kisses on your breast like voters in the hallway
Kisses on your breast like fate
Kisses on your breast like static from a radio
Kisses on your breast like shells from a shoe
Kisses on your breast like princes from a boxing ring
Kisses on your breast like April from a breeze
Kisses on your breast like sauce from a pot
Kisses on your breast like arms around your waist
Kisses on your breast like a man from New York
Kisses on your breast like chairs in a forest
Kisses on your breast like sighs from a sleeper
Kisses on your breast like a plane from a cloud
Kisses on your breast like babies from a ward
Kisses on your breast like tension in a girder
Kisses on your breast like an afternoon
Kisses on your breast
Kisses on your breast like fever from a coffee
Kisses on your breast like sheets from a basket
Kisses on your breast like fire in a pan

Madison Square

1
The squirrel
leaning down the tree
has stopped looking
up and dropped
something
from his front paws.
He puts them
back on the tree
and comes down.

2
The coupled black-coat
couple on the bench là-bas
has gotten undone
and gone by.
They stand behind
a pine tree.

3
In the dog run the little dogs make noise
While the big brown dogs look around.

4
A plastic bag flies from a tree.
A concrete bench wears a scarf.

5
Two squirrels hunch
on a trembling branch.
A dalmatian jumps
with his legs in the air.

Poem

The ink we dignify
what camera-heavy
dictaphone as charged up
framboise wolf in shine
jabber consolable macaronis
floozy-letch totally system

it vacuums spurious
cantatas for local script
nunchuks, clack farms
for fat-fingered readiness
photographs in certain
horizontal pause swans

reading the grid portends
is arbitrary pouts
for mix of toggled
triplicate gurney gaga
soon lessen the toro
fabulous snowdown

The Apparatus Through Which One Can View Any York

So that these are not just words and you,
Sweet and Low, will know what I mean
on any cold Saturday in August, when
any one would be eighteen, New York is
and you are your words such as clearly,
context, and I'm these diagrams spoken
out about, the flowers of culture, and if
dignity means a lot to me so does linguistics.
So do? Let's listen to the Finnish girls
as they correct our French. I like the way
you talk, omitting articles, like a Yiddish
girl. I hear the champions del mundo talking
about themselves, the south, what people
say and seem like, snappy year as evening
comes through, the trees are different
colors, the Louise Bourgeois show closed
and I didn't get there in time, under the
Triboro bridge a poet is jumping in the glass,
twenty years ago a poet-entomologist jumped
from the Bourne Bridge, should a word have
two meanings? What the fuck for
is a line by the dead D. Boon, there are
other people I mean. It's like when someone
says something that surprises, is true,
the light distributes through the smoke a blank
look chases, then see.

Red Mark

the ked soles of the long-haired girl to my right
are wearing down   the river's dark

A Movie Tarpaulin

strung above the yard
twenty meters long
and catching the movies

Flub Grid

My boff itinerary on the blotter,
the postmen in the street on Sunday
deactivate the snipe, the literal blah
of the Iditarod obelisk snobs—
corroborate, comprehend—

Unfinished Question

Past the armistice, on through the party
of the reset brassiere and the star bay
until having surveyed the pastries
and the ashtrays, done the stoichiometry
of esteem and the pesach of tests ...

Uncle, I'm Cold

"No, no, below me!"
A nominal we-mean-well
and the rostrum strewn with culottes untold—
hunky dory, Lord,
more flood, more school.
The mole scrolled the mormon screen
to hoard a Bull Run nickel—
the hunted cuff of a New Jersey nut
its tunneled antiphonal.

Beta Beat Theater

As an invitation to question rage.
Fess-up to sodality and soteriology,
the ravenous genie of your *de jure* siege
stages Mossad mess-up sessions
to test your vim and goose a *Praeterita*
out of you.

Elementary School Banners

To feel menthol
of beam as other
the sham sea
in the nobler data
tall and blank
of fatal blame
the daft marble
as a label daughter
puts on her gaol shades
o morning carnation.

Star Form Stride

I'm starting to feel, that's all.
A rainy night on the firth—
Cha Cha Sousaphone says,
stay and fight the false rain,
feel plain,
but in my yen for stag
I'm a deaf fado singer.
The change thing is a far faster chain
than the confident cruciform salon demesne
finds edifying. I want the foreign rights.
I want editing tape.

Eleven Forgiven

A pirate in a repeat environment
plays tag in the ironing.
Entangle the raiments.
Peeved, tap clogs,
the livery of pillory talk
evangel living as foreign
as the driver of the Rangers' van.
Drying, grieve,
vend the dove in hand
to a liar ring for an Ellery Queen.
England is davening.

Chippewa Mishegas

The Dean of Roses in his crowded prose
delivers the code of Poland
as the search truck
plays its corroded polo:
reroute Jose.
I lost my surf map at the peer dance;
at the freedom mass I had to defy syrup.
I found your seedy trap
of spondee beer—
may you curl March ale in a quaker rescue deal.
Cheers, Dean,
squander your Chicago in a rear-dash crater shocker.
I'll research your snack claim.

Layla Playland

Free sin! The freesia of fight songs
is the only referent on the grief train,
and the twofer of light's laws asks for her.
The scene czar takes the serum—
home run derby in the emergency room.
Outside, the drag actuary takes a monkey deduction,
"Germany, sir, on my bird honor."
The effendi has his cake rations
and I would fain seek thee, Layla Playland,
but the phaser of fantastic urges got me,
or was it our Fergus of Zagreb,
the nose grab, the folk dance.
Come, ply the roars, lady,
my lady so light.

Anecdote Room

for Ron Rice

I have a cat looking in my eyes
(so much for consensus),
the music of Ravel leafleting the dictators
to promote the amaryllis—
do you think it cares stupidly, as if free will
were a catalog to be ordered from
desperate to be turned around and kissed
and a lot more but not here, not now,
not any other time either?
Then give me a deep shot of the water
moving objects by, and the boat
with the Queen of Sheba
and behind her foggy Sheba City
putting the strict back
in the district, don't you think etymology
ought to be more like a library
or a bar, anyplace you can get
turned on by accident on purpose.
And now my time is perforated,
I need a story, I need you to read
to me something not about finance
but redolent of the piano work
I'd train myself in, get laid up to
be tended to by you
better than I could do.

Hold on to Your Light Source

Worthy of its stars and its cold
worthy of the gopher safety of the barge
Change desks and sailing sheaves
Hearing the orders and going into the hive
little minutes shed their casein blazes
I am housing this loss for masquerade swallows
which exhibit their dignities as silent barks

Performance manufactures madness everyday
closeout manchurias. Please love me further
I want something

What Is That What That Is

I give up it's fall
listening to the love of anything
say some cliché I have a crush
The train goes by with a boom

A single tree on the cliffs is red
Women in ads look sad
They're not beautiful but you are
you and the river
The river is burning green

I am not decent! I'm no authority!
I'm caught like a cat

Yeah, No

echolocate
the chocolate

Beer for a Person Believed Lost

No one home but
no one homeless

O unwanted jazz

I see waves
of days on playgrounds—

W

You don't want
aesthetics to be
the only one in the family
knows how to drive

9, a Maze

New darkness of morning a dizzy swindle
I went to the window the navy sky over the street
Nobody walked an orange corridor
posted with traffic lights changing
The window was cold I kissed her forehead red
in the light of the alarm clock where before breakfast the train
pulses along wires overhead in my bag
socks underpants a math book a notebook
The cities stop and start oh la pauvre

Your twelve grand turns up as twenty-four
and there's a Kandinsky in the kitchen
in the hallway in the bathroom
a flashy sombre rhapsody for talk radio
that's poisoned you with expertise
I always feel that a poem I read and suddenly love
because suddenly understanding
is overlooked I've overlooked it
when

Silver
beads on the wrist of scary man in coffeeshop
possibly novelist he loves his hair
Here's a man who smiles his direct hit a microchip
Earring on a woman in plaid she gets up to get milk
her jaw is big she stretches it
What she wanted to do in Ghana was she saved up a lot of
    money and
she wanted to have a lot of clothes made and then she went to
    England

She chooses really bad in the men dept.

Two tables over three days later Cruz's poem is so good
and clear and sad and sometimes it skids, ah work trouble is
    boring
Maureen Owen reads tonight, and Elinor Nauen, the snow
    shines on
in places and goes out, headlights show kicked peaks along the
    sidewalk
Having a good question is a poet's flag of scarves
stitched silently your name drops it's fearless to be bright red
and clear in Philadelphia where we collage blamelessly
Our grist   o holy precision
I'm silently touched
                by your marble enthusiasm

Mid-Atlantic

To feel as you swim through it
that your summer is with its shoulder

Blackbird hovering into a cold ocean
wind turns aside and goes back

some songs
some parts of songs

No Second Seventh and Second

I want to live in that leopard there
male and female like
the flowering margin of the dark.

If it has one place
it is a mountain.

Antique gauloise
rocking horse,
Summer's smashed blonde

Only an ugly
bastard of gruel,

marsh and fog or bright the skin—
not, how does the game work.

A Little Gold, a Second Song

Up off the ground to the left
throwing the sun changing its name
down Seventh past Tenth past Bleecker
Cars sock at the mouth
Some breezes on the shining bar of soap
The steam coming into the hall
I'm going back into the sky to where my mother was born

Folded church programs on the floor the nib of afternoon
and when I get up blood pinching the gold bandages
The air conditioner works and works
The bed a book as big as a room
turns to gold on the terrible street
The turquoise of dawn is painted on the cornice
I want to run behind the barrier

The water in white marigolds gauze
poor room seen in a bowl a school in July
Come pick up the 8-ball
of snow black as a cab and in sunglasses alone again
The magazines in the coffee shop rubber-stamped
jack-o'-lanterns on fire escapes
One hand on the handlebars one hand holding up the guitar

Girl on the corner brought by the octave
time waving snakes go faster!
The baby in the driveway sits up
an ice cream truck plying the air
Don't tell me that's the way the blood in the cloth is
The steering wheel my sunburn healed

city hall dancers on the book of doom

The walls put gold penpoints on the back of my head
I called you north star but I needed to lie down in gold boats
wrote poems bought with gold for any flower to climb
I never saw the ocean come up through the floor
a cloud in the intersection
and the light bending through the ceiling with your cat
The rope rubbing your eye the street door like a hand in your
    hair

All that fever of being caught
That's just the love of the world without you to listen
Music dreams of you
going so fast I have to go to the museum
Please write down the black spark glasses flying
breathing brick on brick with fires
complaining sunlight

Rain on the roads of the recent past
What did I lose? Tiptoes to flood! And you? More than a
    dollar
but sweet and easy pants come off
but not smoke on the fold the biblical violin magnums
cleaned with gold clatter wardens distraught sieve lets rabbits
age into their veins pink buttons and fifty cigars
So much changed like a rose alone!

And light a match to start the day
expecting gray fire of little flowers to sweat and shine

snuggling and slipping to move papers
The difference staring down bathers in the morning
to be washed to the bone glitter hello the seam
Lessons roar forward the scream of the news
You cry the sun alcohol busting asks

Hold my hand the summer separating rain from the viola
and Trafalgars from tetragrammata in the morning
Running in the dirt the home of the poem little zinnias
down streets built of marble and canvas wiving new pasts
of future late afternoons in August crayon'd by weddings
asking the number of rooms brightly stocking
luscious and cold nerves as pilgrims to loathsome stone

The basketball under the trees
newspaper gone crazy on a park bench the long park walk
Asleep I wadded a stop sign into the trash
That's cannonfire this blank July paper flattens out
and that's a tooth red line a garnet tumbled
light through leaves on a propeller plane
under the copper breeze

Maybe that's enough loud telephone chess and mild death
        maybe enough
ideal points of sugar in hard damnation enough newspaper of
        mouth
maybe winds enough driving at night enough clam shell on
        the chest
enough skating on the flood floating tulip enough marking the
lacrosse abominations falling colored air like an arm enough

where the flames crashed overhead good and bad and
	hazelnut paradox
damaged melody of blizzard canal decades and elements
	menstruating
me and you not physical or temporary horns in the sun sailing
chains of grease biplanes novels nature lullabies bars
enough just enough adorable come and go keys enemies and
	clothes
enough sun and moon eating paper almond storms elsewhere
	rolling
on a lemon like a bruise piercing traffic silent churches blazing
black and red enough ranting to power and keeping quiet
	until you
die enough once again and enough no more

It's funny to still get nervous
across this great red land to be a pattern
I'll pour water down the mountain
I can see all the kingdoms from this hill
Bitter bleach and knotty pine mosquito kingdoms
the palace of drums beating horoscopes
I hear but cannot see the courtiers crouching

Their songs are extra to voluptuousness
their endless lazy surrender brings the world its fire
Sleep in love with ink on thumb
a scarf of a black knot yourself a silver stroll in cork
The cool land of diagrams of evening and its starry forelock
Its first song pointing to justice
Its second song "Breathe radiant halo of dark rehearsal

"The game preached by sun on a watch
"By force and old pages in the daisies
"Do you know what you love?
"Close your eyes to the black river
"There was the wind and there were trees
"A bracelet lighting the party
"There were people passing by."

The water alone is comforting
My face on my hand
Fragile sky in the ugly city you see on tv
place on the knob a set of keys
that day begin
to sing a shaped poem
of the fall of the water and the light from the sky

Étude

The original ray sped off,
clear brunt on Brooklyn air.

A sifting factory is here.
I'm wet as an umbrella,

Loyalty, kielbasy, low roofs,
a glove

floats down from the top floor.
Inside is the key

and then fuzz is on the land, ominous
thudding down the track is flooded

If you get that right, that look—
If you pay attention completely for once

defending its low reverse
into island musics to no mainland.

The old money burns holes in old maps
like a puppet in the light.

Angel bending in the smoke
to reach a dollar coin.

The secluded dome of pressure,
chalked lines of truck panels,

To be comfortable with it
is a level, that is, a bubble.

Theatrical nature in stripes
adjusts itself to the page

a cat's thigh. A bus parks like snow
across the street, white, reflective,

I have some sensitivities, and prompt
as stimuli they occupy me, then turn.

And wander not away, but, born
in loud pathos of a sill,

under the light streetlight,
in the blue extended shadow of a spark,

wander to the bottom of the tap.
Scarf! Proud piccolo of winter's interviewing

throat. To find the poem,
darken the tulips

and fold over the light of the water.
The machine of it shrugs meaning,

willingly walks the slip in sweatpants
tenancy imposes and sleep condones,

large reddish British girl,
the precipice of history awaits!

Rigor shouts "Feel!"
but it is a suede of yourself

the stuff of color winches.
Language closes

lockets. Passers-by, just walking
toward a lily. In the limbo

of anything but bells, the playground's bed,
sumptuous and yawning, spare heather

eyeglasses slick like script in the rain.
These afternoons are sold to order,

each line schedules fine apologies of beads,
common phantoms.

The drug endures
on broken caulk and the infant

in the doorway alike—
The forest the doorway is

when one unknown steps there,
the doorbell buzzes with indentations.

Poem

I heard a bee
and I walked into the ocean

The roses had all been cleared

The purple body of a jellyfish went by
and as the sun set to my right

I climbed out of the water awkwardly like a dog

Flying over the River

the currents. I drove along with my scissors.
mustard-colored luggage, she could cook—

this was the city I'd heard so much
underground. The fire appeared to be

fine. How are you doing? At oblique
angles, oblongs recycle the everybody

at night with the succulents. Be polite
to travel across the network massage

they have reason to believe it's code. I'm not.
I follow it by instruments and life doesn't

inherited it. Maybe later we could
speaking with one voice about urgent matters.

Hommage à Jean-Pierre Leaud

The present tense is neither sincere
nor insincere; although it's occupied
by a window washer with eyes like
cleaning fluid, the place called here
is the last best proxy for home—
and as when you are eight or nine
the secrets that bring relaxation
are feats of sleight of hand
slipping out of chinese handcuffs.
Tell yourself to listen to what you know,
show up, stand where they tell you,
move your face as little as necessary—
Smile and pout and time and space'll
make you miss your train.

Surcharge Turnkey

so densely
I'm walking around
the finish spirit
and afterwards *let's*
do that
the fraying of *yes*
again
before it's started *let's*
do that again

The Unmistakeable Children's-Book Quality

The taste test inside you generates votes
against democracy, and in the heat waves, even,
they're advocating a truth-seeming different
indeed from truth serum. Wave back with me as I say
the business of America is anybody's, and therefore
nobody's, and I sit through the indoctrination
twice or three times, in the rocking chairs
deep inside the death star, to get my worth.
It could be right the first time, it could
be written, but nobody speaks to me
and I am used to the way the room gets bright
when the breeze off the river turns the trees
in the courtyard. Paper slides under door.

Think Tank Girl

Do the easy things first, get some momentum.
It's a management principle. Also?
You might make sure you're not poisoning apples
in the sprawl, claiming responsibility
for turning the hillside from smooth dark green
to a grid of pale cubes, an avocado
you'd invert to feed your young.
In a free market they call sneak attacks troubleshooting.

You could stare into the data with an earnest face
and fail to generalize
except to see a Persian rug in it and (steganography
as persistence error) eyes and a circle, an open mouth.
Whether it does it quickly
by cutting off your most sensitive part—your future—
or whether it walls off the part of your brain
that cloaks your feelings to let you breathe,

the thing you think you live for kills you.
That, as far as I know, is the reasonable
connection between love and death; it works
For all x. Think-tank girl, you have the right idea:
can't be a free agent
until you've starred on a team.
Get carrying those cartons of leaflets.
No shame there, Defoe wrote them too.

The painted jar of peaches, wax paper
over the top, will not always be
at the top of the stair, the couple

kissing on the landing is mentally in Samarkand
and can the third thing
be kept at bay, uncomprehending ally,
for as long as the consolidation takes?
Maybe, if the money's betting on you.

If you cornered me on that teacher joke,
What separates us from the animals?
I'd answer with the animals: a fence.
The CEOs agree, put down books.
You need a bias to action, a point of view
animating you into argument. Hint:
Safety in numbers only overlaps with love.
If you want a guide, there are two: gold and rule.

Long Pauses between Cakes

I'm not sensitive
I just notice everything
and remember it
forever. And then
there are the ideas
those everything-covering
details suggest—
how many years they've kept
as bribes
not to appear. Not to be
the Brazilian flag but
how many months have you gone
without cleaning the light
out of your playacting?
The giggle in the carburetor
is telling. It is a figleaf.
The boo in book.

Coming Soon

I knock on the door as I turn my key
but there's no answer except the scratch
across the floor of the Boston Terrier,
so solid, so ugly, so curious, so polite.
10:30, or so it says on the VCR
in the lit front room. The kitchen/bedroom
is dark, and silent. Are Todd and Carrie out
for the night, or just out? It is spring,
and it is snowing, and the wind chime
in the street is so persistent I half expect
to see a glockenspiel being played by a monkey
in a little cap—but no, only crushed cans.
I don't hear any breathing, or other sleep noise.
It's 10:43, and somehow I am still me.

Periphrase

You are beautiful and I wish you would have children.
When you are old, it would make you happy to have them.
You owe it to your mother, who was as beautiful as you.
If you die, there won't be anyone with your beauty around.
You are going to get old and die, you know.
Give it up! You should have ten kids.
Do you think you'll just come back, like the sun?
Is this music bothering you?
I don't buy that you're afraid of leaving a widow behind.
I think you hate yourself; prove me wrong.
As you get older, your child will be young.
Really, having a kid is as close as you can get to eternal youth.
Think of it as good business.
I don't need to know your sign, I can see it in your eyes.

People are like plants; I'm trying to get you to propagate,
but I can't do it just with poetry—
and by the way unless you have a child nobody's going to
     believe how beautiful I say you are.
Well … you are beautiful, and I'm a pretty good poet.
I want to tell time not to let you get old.
God! It's too bad neither of us is a woman.
I hope I never say dippy things in praise of you.
When we're together I don't feel older than you.
Sometimes I get so excited with you that I say crazy things—
     ignore them.
For example, when I said "bosom shop" I was just frustrated.
I don't want to be president, I only want your vote (or, to vote
     for you? I'm confused),

and I wish you'd say something so I could tell you how much
    I love you.
Even when I'm worn out, thoughts of you keep me up,
day and night—I need to get some! And to give

And I feel pretty low until I remember that you love me—
I'll cry over everything that ever made me sad, then I'll
    remember you,
your chest (among other things) reminding me of my whole
    scorecard.
When I'm gone, if you read my poems, I know there are better
    poets, but which ones loved you more?
Hey, did you just go behind a cloud? Where'd you go?
I don't care that you're back, that hurt!
Gosh, it didn't hurt that much—cheer up.
It was probably my fault. It was absolutely my fault.
You make an old poet happy.
With you around, there's always something to write about.

Evasion of Privacy

When they ask me can they just be honest,
the sweetest place I can go is out to flash cards
I watched come up over the hills
then go behind a cloud until dusk,
a word that settles on marigolds
with intent to bioluminesce. *Just
leave me alone* means *come home
and love me,* I thought everyone knew.

What Feelings Are For

I thought I was running as hard
as possible, but now I'm going faster
it feels better, actually.

Something is pushing me
through a translucent membrane toward the sky.
I can't quite see the sharp edges of clouds
but I am tumbling uncomfortably
toward this blue and white upper limit,
rolling up on a wave of garbage—

The neuroses of animals are all
that keep us from full-on interspecies war.

Acknowledgments

Some of these poems appeared in earlier forms in the following publications:

American Poet, Cocodrilo, Court Green, DC Poetry, Explosive, Fence, Fort Necessity, H_NGM_N, Lingo, Mississippi Review, Purple, Saginaw, Shiny, Talisman, Thrush, Wax Nine, The World, and the chapbooks *Always-Already, Hidden Poems, A Little Gold Book, Noise, Upstairs,* and *Yeah, No.*

Thanks to Marc Vincenz, and to David Blair who introduced us.

I want to acknowledge the presence in these poems of Xeni Fragakis, Max Winter, Anna Malmude, Jo Brahinsky, Robert V. Hale, Stephen Malmude, Sandy Mowbray-Clarke, Christopher Edgar, David Shapiro, Kenneth Koch, Michael Friedman, Lewis Warsh, Keston Sutherland, Andrea Brady, Gary Sullivan, Gary Stanton, Tom Orange, and the Subpoetics group, all of whom commented on, and in some cases knowingly or unknowingly collaborated with me on, early versions of these poems. I also want to thank Sadie Dupuis, David Harrison Horton, rob mclennan, and Sam Riviere.

Thanks to Yael for her general enthusiasm, and her patience with this project.

Thanks also to Charles North, Joshua Weiner, and Kate Colby; and incalculable thanks to Charles for his consideration of, and interventions in, these versions. The errors that remain are mine.

About the Author

JORDAN DAVIS is the author of two previous collections of poetry: *Million Poems Journal* (Faux Press, 2003) and *Shell Game* (Edge Books, 2018). His poems have appeared in *Poetry, American Poetry Review,* and the *New Yorker;* his prose has appeared in *Slate, Boston Review,* and the *Times Literary Supplement;* he was the inaugural columnist for *Fence Magazine*'s Constant Critic website. With Chris Edgar he co-edited *The Hat, Teachers & Writers,* and a short-lived iOS poetry app called *Ladowich.* He has also edited *The Poetry Project Newsletter* and the poetry section of *The Nation.* He is a founding editor of the Subpress Collective, was associated with the Flarf poets, and hosted several reading series in New York, including Poetry City and the Million Poems Show. He co-edited several volumes of the selected and collected works of Kenneth Koch.